THE JFK REPERTO

PRESEN

BY
STEPHANIE McKNIGHT

ff

faber and faber

JFK was set up by Karen Louise Hebden and Bruce Athol MacKinnon and officially launched at the Royal National Theatre in June 1995, after receiving an award from The Snipe Charitable Trust.

We aim for artistic excellence at all times, creating a rich and fertile base from which the British Theatre will reap an exciting, diverse, artistically driven and challenging harvest.

JFK commissioned and produced **Darktales** by Tim Arthur first at The Pleasance, Edinburgh in 1995, and then transferring an expanded version into The Arts, London, in 1996.

Our current three-year programme is visionary because it looks to the future and dares to say there is a better way to produce the next generation of theatre practitioners. The industry cannot continue to condemn these young people to a life of poverty, working in cramped, unsafe fringe venues, where their work will be restricted by the total lack of resources both in terms of time, money and equipment.

These young artists are expected to speak to the few, not because their voices lack vision or talent, but because many of the spaces that are available to them are tiny, and the money they have to realise their visions is often non-existent.

Through the next three years, **JFK** will release these voices and talents, allowing them to speak to the many, and create a new and vibrant future for British Theatre.

JFK is dedicated to a future that is healthy and bright for both our theatre practitioners and audiences.

JFK is a member of the Independent Theatre Council
JFK is a registered charity, No. 1054950

Cast (*in order of appearance*)

REB	Linda Marlowe
LUCAS	Benedick Bates
EDWIN	John Hasler
DORY	Peta Lily
NICK	Robert Gill

Directed by	Karen Louise Hebden
Designed by	Bruce Athol MacKinnon
Music / Sound Score by	Stephen Edwards
Fights Directed by	Terry King
Lighting Designed by	Will Scarnell
Sound Designer	Nick Gilpin

Production Manager	Theatre Futures
Associate Designer	Stuart David Nunn
Stage Manager	Nicki Courtenay
Assistant Stage Manager / Props	Dawn Travis
Sound Operator	Henrietta Cooper
Assistant Stage Manager	Nicki Courtenay
Set Built by	Mushroom Construction (0171 278 3272)
Production Photographer	Jaap Buitendijk (0958 407 171)
Graphics Design	Katya Kroeger
Copywriter	Paul Moulton

Stephanie McKnight (Author)

Stephanie McKnight's first play **Beat the Air** was produced at the Finborough Arms Theatre in 1993. She was subsequently awarded the Arts Council Playwriting Bursary and was given development money by the Hampstead Theatre to write her second play **The Cub**. Commissioned by the Royal Court Young People's Theatre, her third play **Dreaming Guns** was produced in August 1995. Stephanie has completed a screenplay **Caterpillars** and is currently writing a commission for BBC Radio and a stage play **Bloodwood**.

Benedick Bates (Lucas)

Trained at LAMDA. Theatre includes: **Fortune's Fool, Simply Disconnected** (Chichester Festival Theatre), the title rôle in **Don Carlos**, **Romeo and Juliet** (Citizen's Theatre, Glasgow), **The Rose Tattoo** (Theatr Clwyd), the title rôle in **The Picture of Dorian Grey** (Gloria Theatre Ltd), **The Return of A.J. Raffles** (Watford Civic Theatre). Film: **Deadly Advice** (Deadly Advice Productions). TV: **Real Women** (BBC).

Robert Gill (Nick)

Trained at Welsh College of Music and Drama. Theatre includes **When We Are Married** (Savoy Theatre), **A Christmas Carol** (Carl Orff Theatre, Munich), **Much Ado About Nothing** (Hysterica Passio Theatre Company, Southwark Playhouse), **The Rivals** (Southwark Playhouse), **Macbeth**, **Woyzeck** (Astra Theatre Company), **Country Dancing** (Theatre in the Downs), **Under Milk Wood** (Mermaid Theatre, Copenhagen), **The Real Long John** (Battersea Arts Centre), **The Last Will and Testament of Popsy Petal** (The Kings Head, Islington), **The Boys in the Band** (Grand Theatre, Swansea). Musicals include **The Boyfriend, Cabaret, Grease, Jesus Christ Superstar, West Side Story, The Wizard of Oz**. TV: **Eastenders, 999** (Series 4).

John Hasler (Edwin)

Trained at Sylvia Young Theatre School. Theatre includes **Mirandola**, **Forty Years On** (Stephen Joseph Theatre, Scarborough), **Conversations with my Father** (Scarborough), **Lost in Yonkers** (Mercury Colchester), **Oliver!** (Crucible Theatre, Sheffield), **Macbeth** (RSC, Barbican). Television includes: **Against All Odds** (BBC), **Harry's Mad II** (Central), **Wonders in Letterland, T-bag Strikes Again, T-bag Bounces Back, Tune into T-bag, T- bag and the Revenge of the T-Set** (all Thames). Film: **Breakout** (Children's Film Foundation).

Peta Lily (Dory)

Theatre includes: **All Over Lovely** (The Traverse and UK Tour), **The Porter's Daughter** (NTC: UK Tour), **Gormenghast** (International Tour), **Charley's Aunt** (Royal Exchange, Manchester), **Low Fidelity, Beg!** (Lily & Co: UK Tour), **Hiroshima Mon Amour, Wendy Darling, Frightened of Nothing, Red Heart, Whole Parts** (all Peta Lily Mime Theatre: UK and International Tours) Directing credits include **The Cat Man's Tail** (Opera Circus), **The Porter's Daughter** (The Cockpit), **Café Ha!** (Nightshift Dance Theatre), **The Wooden Boy, Rites and Lies** (The Guizers).

Linda Marlowe (Reb)

Recent theatre includes: **The Misanthrope** (Young Vic), **Silverface** (Gate Theatre),

900 Oneonta (Lyric Theatre, Hammersmith), **Through the Leaves** (Leicester Haymarket), **Oedipus Trilogy, The Virtuoso, Twelfth Night** (all RSC), **Ghost Sonata** (QEH), **A Flea in her Ear, Too Clever by Half** (Old Vic), **A Streetcar Named Desire** (Sherman Theatre). She has worked extensively with Steven Berkoff including **Decadence, Metamorphosis, Hamlet, Greek, The Trial** and most recently the international tour of **Coriolanus**. Recent television includes: **Silent Witness, The Tenant of Wildfell Hall, She's Out, Class Act, Love Hurts, A Pinch of Snuff, The Green Man**. Film includes: **The James Gang, Fever, Manifesto, Mr Love, Snake Eyes, Dynamo, Tamlyn**. Directing credits include: **Mensch Meier, The Artificial Jungle, Through the Leaves** (all Leicester Studio), **The Games Rule, High Brave Boy** (RSC Festival, King's Head), **Metamorphosis** (Contact Theatre, Manchester), **A View from the Bridge, A Madhouse in Goa** (Oldham Coliseum Theatre).

Production Team

Karen Louise Hebden (Director)

Graduated from Newcastle upon Tyne with a degree in English. She has directed **Darktales** (The Arts Theatre, London, The Pleasance, Edinburgh), **Company, Annie** and **Hayfever** (Playhouse Theatre, Newcastle), **Fragments of a Dream** (Riverside Studios) and **The Hanuman** (White Bear). After training at RADA, she was Assistant Director at the West Yorkshire Playhouse to Jude Kelly on **Taming of the Shrew** and Matthew Warchus on **Fiddler on the Roof**. Whilst there she also directed a rehearsed

reading of **Rosencrantz and Guildernstern are Dead** (Courtyard Theatre). She is Artistic Director of **The JFK Repertory Company** and a Director of **Thoor Productions** which is bringing the new musical **Myst** into the West End in Autumn1998. **Darktales** tours nationally from 17 September 1997: opening at Cambridge Arts Theatre.

Bruce Athol MacKinnon (Designer)

Holds a Postgraduate Diploma in Theatre Design (CSSD). He has designed **Darktales** (The Arts Theatre, London, UK Tour, The Pleasance, Edinburgh), **The Winter's Tale** (Vanbrugh Theatre), **Fragments of a Dream** (Riverside Studios), **Death of a Salesman** (Centenary Theatre), **Loot, Faith, Hope & Charity** and **One for the Road** (all Embassy Studio), **The Hanuman** (White Bear), the award winning productions **After their Loving** and **1959 Pink Thunderbird** (Man in the Moon), Sondheim's musical **Sweeney Todd** (Cluny, Edinburgh), and the ballet **Romeo and Juliet** (Arts Council Theatre Designers Exhibition). He assisted Anthony Ward on **The Winter's Tale, The Virtuoso, The Alchemist** (RSC), and the double bill **Yolande** and **The Nutcracker** (Opera North/AMP). He is Associate Director of **The JFK Repertory Company** and a Director of **Thoor Productions**. He is designing **Myst** the musical: opening Autumn 1997.

Stephen Edwards (Composer)

Currently working on a musical adaptation of **Tess of the D'Urbervilles** in collaboration with Keith Dewhurst (rehearsed reading, Old Vic). His previous opera and music theatre works include **Accidental Miracles** (Sydney Theatre Company/ WAAPA) directed by David Freeman, **Crystal Balls** (Eastern Touring Agency tour/ Sadlers Wells), **The Ninth Wonder** (Sydney Theatre Company), all three in collaboration with Justin Fleming. **Four Baboons Adoring The Sun,** a collaboration with John Guare (Lincoln Center, New York), **Trackers of Oxyrhynchus,** a collaboration with Tony Harrison (Delphi Festival, Royal National Theatre, European Tour and Sydney Theatre Company), and **Kafka's Trial** a collaboration with Lynne Williams (Darlington Festival). Scores for film and TV directed by Peter Hall include **Camomile Lawn** (C4), **Orpheus Descending** (Turner Films), and **She's Been Away** (BBC). Previous music/sound scores for theatre include **Darktales** (Arts Theatre) for The JFK Repertory Company, **A Streetcar Named Desire** (Haymarket Theatre), **Hamlet** (Gielgud Theatre), **The Rose Tattoo** and **Twelfth Night** (West End's Playhouse Theatre), and **Orpheus Descending** (Haymarket Theatre and Neal Simon Theatre, Broadway) all for Peter Hall Theatre Company, **Cymbeline, A Winter's Tale** and **The Tempest** (all RNT), **Kafka's Castle, Come the Revolution** and **As You Like It** for Cherub Theatre Company, London. Orchestral works include **A Triple Concerto Ménage à Trois for Marimba, Trumpet and Vibraphone with Orchestra** and **Brickfields Lament a Concerto for Orchestra** premièred by the BBC Symphony Orchestra conducted by Oliver Knussen. He has been commissioned by The JFK Repertory Company to write **Letter to Felice**, a lyrical work about Franz Kafka.

Will Scarnell (Lighting Designer)

Lighting designs include **Sweeney Todd, The Erpingham Camp, The White Room, Cyrano de Bergerac, Barney Bay and Trip Marley's Blacklight Circus, Noises Off, Grease** (all Uppingham Theatre), **The Faerie Queen** (Harrow Theatre), **New Child Sexuality, Feet Across the Sea** (Turtle Key), **The Gravity Swing** (UK and US Tour), **Wilde Tales** (UK Tour), **Amadeus** (UK Tour).

Nick Gilpin (Sound Designer)

Nick joined Autograph in 1986 after a brief period in concert sound. He subsequently worked as Assistant Sound Designer on the West End productions of **The Sneeze, The Cherry Orchard, Metropolis, Look Look, Just So, Five Guys Named Moe, City of Angels, In The Midnight Hour** (UK Tour), **Miss Saigon** (Stuttgart, Seattle and Scheveningen) and **Martin Guerre**. As Sound Designer he has been responsible for **Hidden Laughter, Private Lives, A Tribute to the Blues Brothers, Eurovision, Indian Ink, Burning Blue, One Word Improv**, Alan Ayckbourn's **Henceforward, Man of the Moment, Revengers Comedies** and **Time of my Life**. He also worked on the Anthony Hopkins/ George Martin production of **Under Milk Wood** which marked the opening of the new Air Studios at Lyndhurst Hall. Nick runs Autograph's recording studio and has been responsible for the sound effects used in productions such as **Into the Woods, Miss Saigon, City of Angels** and **Hair**.

He has worked on several radio productions including the award winning documentary **Partners in Crime**.

THEATRE FUTURES
(Production Managment)

Theatre Futures is primarily a company of theatre consultants and designers. Current work includes the refurbishment of The Opera House, Jersey, and a new theatre for **Cumbria Theatre Trust**. Recently **Dan Watkins** and **Anthony Alderson** of Theatre Futures have formed a new division which focuses on production services and project management for the entertainment industry. Recent and current work includes production management for the West End runs of **Darktales**

(JFK: Arts Theatre), **David Strassman** (Apollo Theatre and tour of Australia and New Zealand), and **Summer Begins** (Donmar Warehouse). Dan is also Production Manager for **Pleasance London** and **Pleasance Edinburgh.**

Stuart David Nunn
(Associate Designer)

Graduated from Nottingham Trent University in June 97 with a BA Honours Degree in Theatre Design. He devised and designed **A Live Bed Show** and has designed **Chaos in the Court of Louis 14** (Live Bait: Nott Dance Festival). He has exhibited at the **New Designers Exhibition** (Design Centre, London). He is Assistant Designer on **Darktales** (JFK: UK tour).

COMMISSIONED PAINTING

In line with its commitment to supporting artists from all areas, **JFK** has commissioned Jonathan Farr to paint the portrait used in the production. Materials sponsored by **Winsor & Newton**.

Jonathan Farr (Commissioned Painter)
Graduated from the Slade School of Fine Art 1997 (BA Hons: Fine Art Sculpture). He has been recently awarded **The Evelyn de Morgan Drawing Prize**, **The 1997 Dolby Travel Award**. He is returning to Barcelona this summer (Art Exchange to Winchester School of Art, Barcelona 1996) prior to travelling to Mexico to study Early Hispanic Art.

Douglas Stewart Ltd is an award winner under the **Pairing Scheme** (the National Heritage Arts Sponsorship Scheme) for its support of **The JFK Repertory Company**.

The Pairing Scheme is a Government Scheme managed by ABSA (Association for Business Sponsorship of the Arts). Pair up with the arts and raise your profile.

Your strategic marketing and PR can be improved by sponsoring the arts. It is one of the most powerful ways to reinforce your corporate image, allowing you to promote your company's name, logo, products and services to a wider, targeted audience. Highly visible and cost-effective, arts sponsorship also gives you the opporunity to develop and strengthen your involvement with the cultural life of your community.

If you receive a Pairing Scheme award, this can also bring valuable Government endorsements, access to influential contacts and help you receive more prominent press coverage.

ABSA manages the Pairing Scheme on behalf of the Department of the National Heritage. If you want to sponsor an arts organisation or event, we could match your sponsorship pound for pound. That means your money goes as far and your business gains double the benefits.

LIFELINERS

is our way of thanking supporters who are the lifeblood of this diverse, exciting and forward-thinking company which will become a rich and fertile launch-pad for the theatre practitioners of the future.

The Lifeliner Schemes are a tax-efficient donation scheme operated by **JFK** to support running costs of the company. They are separated into five subheadings: Platinum £5000+, Gold £2500+, Silver £1000+, Bronze £500+, Lifeliner £ other

Corporate Lifeliners

PLATINUM £5000   **Eurotunnel plc**

GOLD £2500   **Marks & Spencer plc**

Incentives include tickets for opening nights, corporate logos in programmes, availability of discounted tickets for company employess and corporate entertaining.

Lifeliner 97 (TO DATE)

BRONZE £500 +   ALAIN BOUBLIL
IAN HOLM
THE SNIPE CHARITABLE TRUST

MARKS & SPENCER

Gold Corporate Lifeliner

PRODUCTION SPONSORS

(at time of going to print)

BAT Industries

20/20 Lens Centre

Big Screen, Cantor + Silver

Moët et Chandon

Wardrobe care by Lever Bros

Winsor & Newton

If you would like to receive further information on **JFK**,
its productions and its commissions please write to
**The JFK Repertory Company, 95 Sutherland Avenue,
Maida Vale, London W9 2HG**

Stephanie McKnight
The Cub

faber and faber
LONDON · BOSTON

First published in 1997
by Faber and Faber Limited
3 Queen Square London WC1N 3AU

Typeset by Country Setting, Woodchurch, Kent TN26 3TB
Printed in England by Intype London Ltd

A CIP record for this book
is available from the British Library

ISBN 0–571–19381–1

2 4 6 8 10 9 7 5 3 1

The kitchen is the heart of the home.
And home is where the heart is.

Characters

Reb (Rebecca) Fifty

Lucas Nineteen

Dory (Dorothy) Late forties

Edwin Sixteen

Nick Mid-fifties

*The action takes place over twenty-four hours
in the kitchen of a middle-class home
in a big city*

Scene One

A comfortable, spacious kitchen. Enough room for a sofa and chairs. Well-equipped, slightly shabby. The family's accumulated artefacts of twenty years. Some rather fine modern pottery items displayed; some paintings and sculptures, mainly African.

Beautiful in its domestic artistry: a blend of light, colour, texture, warmth, informality. Beautifully clean.

Fishing tackle in one corner.

Somewhat out of keeping with the aesthetics of the room, on a stand in a corner, is a computer – keyboard, screen, software, etc.

The centrepiece is a large kitchen table.

Other rooms lead off.

Open French doors lead into a lovely wild garden at the centre back.

It is summer. Hot. Midnight.

Evidence of cooking. A huge jug of raspberry ice-cream in the making stands on the table, egg cartons, cream containers, beaters, etc.

Modern jazz playing softly from a tape deck.

Reb stands absolutely motionless in an advanced yoga pose.

She wears wide-bottomed shorts and a brief tee-shirt. Comfortable, but arty.

5

This is her life. Her world.

She shifts into the matching pose on the other leg.

A moment or two, then she lies on the floor relaxing.

A moment or two, then she gets up. Goes to the ice-cream mixture. Tastes it. Thinks. A dash of fruit liqueur. Tastes again.

Feels the side of the jug – still warm. Clears up. Goes to French doors and steps out into garden. Stands and looks up at the sky for a moment. Disappears into garden. Sound of hosepipe running and some watering. Turns it off. Comes back in with a few sprigs of herbs. Crushes a few leaves in her fingers and smells with delight. Lovingly puts the remainder in a little pot. Feels jug again. Gets out electric ice-cream maker. Pours mixture in. Turns it on.

Looks at watch. Turns off music. Turns off lights apart from one small one by the French doors. Goes out of room, stepping out of shorts. Sound of teeth being cleaned. Shower running. It stops. Footsteps padding into another room. Creak of bed. Silence.

Time passes.

A young man suddenly appears at the French doors. He wears a black polo sweater, jeans, Doc Marten boots, a black stocking over his face and black leather gloves. He stands listening intently. Then comes in stealthily. Looks and listens at all the doors leading off. Nothing. All quiet. Stands in kitchen looking around. Looking for something specific. He doesn't find it. Takes in ice-cream maker. Looks inside. Smells. Takes off one glove. Sticks finger in. Rolls up stocking a little way. Licks it. No reaction. Puts glove back on. Starts looking in drawers. Finds large kitchen knife. Takes it and goes toward bedroom. Stops.

Goes back to drawers. Hunts again. Finds large serving spoon. Goes to ice-cream maker. Puts down knife. Sits.

Takes spoonful. Rolls up stocking. Eats. And another. And another. A few more. Turns off ice-cream maker. Leaves the spoon. Rolls down stocking. Picks up knife again. Goes off to bedroom. A moment.

(Off.) Sound of woman screaming in fear. Suddenly cut off as hand goes over her mouth.

Lucas *(off – voice muffled by stocking)* If you scream lady I'll cut your fingers off.

Silence.

Where's your money?

Sound of woman crying.

Shut up. I just want your handbag.

Sound of crying gets louder. Sound of face being slapped. Small scream. Then silence.

I told you. The money.

Reb *(off – her voice faint)* The kitchen. Somewhere.

A moment. Reb darts into the kitchen. Wearing a nightgown. Runs to the furthest corner. Lucas follows. She cowers. He watches her from the doorway. She looks wildly round the room. Sees open French doors. Telephone. He holds up knife.

She whimpers. Searches for handbag. Finds it. She opens it. Takes out wallet. Takes out money and hands it over to him. He indicates her watch. She hands that over. He indicates chain around her neck. She is reluctant. He insists. She hands it over.

A long moment.

Something in her demeanour changes. She looks at him intently. At his body. At his clothes.

Finally at his boots.

7

Reb I've cleaned those boots.

Long moment.

He looks down at them.

He looks at the money and jewellery.

Puts it in his pocket, turns, and goes towards the French doors.

Lucas?

He has his back turned. He grips the knife and half raises it. A salutation? A warning?

Suddenly she runs after him. Staggers. Puts her hands on his shoulders. As if on the point of collapse. Feels her way down his back. Puts her hands on his waist and holds him. Stopping him from going into the garden. He holds his arms out to the side, still with the knife.

I'd recognise that lovely body anywhere.

They stand.

You really scared me.

She hugs him to her. Starts to cry.

I thought you were going to . . .

He twists lightly out of her embrace. Rips the stocking from his head.

Lucas You should be so lucky.

Reb It's you. I'm just so glad. (*Pause.*)
What a dreadful feeling.

He waggles his backside at her.

Lucas Recognise my bum, did you?

8

Turns. Thrusts his pelvis at her.

Lucas   Recognise this?

Reb   Don't be tiresome.

He opens the fridge, snacks on odd bits of food, finds a bottle of champagne. Takes it out.

Lucas   What's all this then? (*Indicates champagne, ice-cream, etc.*)

Reb   You should know.

Lucas   Would I ask?

Reb   It's the 24th tomorrow.

Lucas   And?

Reb   My birthday.

Lucas   Yeah?

Reb   My fiftieth.

Lucas   Is it?

Reb   You know about it.

Lucas   Do I?

Reb   Nick's coming home.

Lucas   God. Dad is? Is he?

Reb   I thought I'd make something special.

Lucas   Because *he's* coming back.

Reb   Well no. Not exactly.

Lucas   I don't like raspberry ice-cream.

Reb   You love raspberry ice-cream.

Lucas   I'd rather have apple pie.

Reb I can make an apple pie. What time is it? We should really go to bed.

Lucas (*sings*) 'Happy Birthday to you.
　Happy Birthday to you.
　I saw a fat monkey
　And I thought it was you.'

Reb Charmed I'm sure.

Lucas Oh, look, Mum. I think you've wet yourself.

Reb gives no physical sign of acknowledgement.

Reb What do you expect? A burglar breaks into your house –

Lucas I didn't break in.

Reb And holds a knife to your throat. He could murder you.

Lucas You're probably in shock. Have a drink. Champagne?

Reb Lucas, no. It's for tomorrow.

Lucas It *is* tomorrow.

He tucks the knife into his boot. Reb offers to put it back. He demurs.

Get out the . . . what are they called?

Reb What?

Lucas You know, Mum. For champagne.

Reb Flutes.

Lucas That's it. Flutes. Get them out.

Reb I don't want any. I'm going to bed.

He opens the bottle.

Lucas   I won't bother with a glass. (*He drinks.*)

Reb   You've had enough.

Lucas   Never enough.

She goes out of the room.

Lucas   (*calling out*) You should get yourself some decent night attire. Man. It doesn't suit you.

Reb returns in shorts and tee-shirt.

Reb   You could have asked me for the money.

Lucas   You could have left it where I could find it.

Reb   What more do you want, Lucas? Blood?

Lucas   Would you have given me some? See? No you would not.

Reb   What was it for?

Lucas   I wanted to buy you a gorgeous, fab present.

Reb   Did you?

Lucas   Only joking.

Reb   I didn't believe you anyway.

Lucas   Actually it's none of your business, is it really?

Reb   I'd like it back. Please.

Lucas   No.

Reb   Please, Lucas. I'm asking you.

Lucas   No way.

Reb   It's all I've got.

Lucas   A bloody lot!

Reb   To see us through the weekend.

Lucas   I have a weekend too you know!

Reb   Can I have my watch. And my necklace.

Silence.

Reb   Have you no common decency?

Lucas   No. (*Pause.*) I blame the mother.

Reb   I'll talk to you in the morning.

She starts to go out. He intercepts her. Takes the necklace and puts it round her neck.

Reb   Thank you.

Gives her back her watch. She puts it on.

Lucas   Please stay.

They stare at each other. She sits up on the table.

He finds a flute for her and pours out a glass of champagne. He toasts her with the bottle.

Reb   You drink too much.

He toasts her again and drinks again.

Reb   I ought to ring the police.

Lucas   You won't.

Reb   What can I say? My son broke into the house. With a black stocking over his face. And threatened me with a knife. Whoever would believe me?

Lucas   Exactly.

Reb   *My* stocking. And my cashmere polo neck.

Lucas   I needed something black.

Reb   You've stretched it.

Lucas   It'll be okay Mum, when you've washed it.

Reb No. It won't. Take it off.

He takes off the sweater. Revealing a bare torso. Hands it to her.

Reb Lucas. It stinks.

Lucas My first burglary. I was shitting myself.

Reb And look. You've torn it under the arms.

Reb begins to cry. Lucas uncomfortable.

Reb Honestly. Why is it always mine?

Lucas Yours are so much softer.

Reb You said you'd cut my fingers off.

Lucas I was thinking about cooking. That it would make it difficult for you to cook. That's all.

Reb attacks him rather feebly. He grabs her by the wrists and holds her off easily.

Reb How dare you do this to me? You little monster. What in God's name is the matter with you?

Lucas Everything I guess.

Reb Bloody right.

Lucas You weren't meant to wake up.

Reb But I did wake up.

Lucas You could have let me go once you knew it was me. Saved us both a lot of aggro.

Reb I should have just said, 'Oh, yeah, it's my son, Lucas the burglar, robbing me. It isn't some kind of practical joke, but it's okay. I don't want to cause embarrassment, or incur his wrath by drawing attention to his odd behaviour. So I'll just let him leave with all my money and personal jewellery. And maybe I'll raise it with him next time I see him.'

Lucas Sort of.

Reb You're crazy.

Lucas I just borrowed your sweater –

Reb No!

Lucas If I were a girl I'd be doing it all the time.

Reb No!

Lucas What's mine is yours in a family. Roughly. Mutual support. You scratch my back and I'll do yours.

Reb Oh, yeah. When?

Lucas Just name the day.

Reb You used to be such a lovely little boy. You had long golden –

Lucas I've heard it all before.

Reb But it's true.

Lucas You were probably a lovely little girl. Once.

Reb What am I going to do with you?

Reb's crying dies away.

Lucas I'm sorry I hit you.

Reb You hit me!

Lucas You hit me!

Reb When?

Lucas Millions of times.

Reb Smacked.

Lucas Hit.

Reb Not like that. You were little.

Lucas Little hits.

Reb No. (*Pause.*) I never liked doing it.

Lucas So why did you?

Silence.

Did you recognise my bum?

Reb Of course not.

Lucas We've got the same legs, don't you think? Maybe that's what you saw.

He sits on the table next to her.

But mine are much longer. Bigger and stronger. As is appropriate for a man.

He swings his legs. Catches sight of boots.

You've never cleaned these ones. You said I should do them myself. On my seventeenth birthday.

Reb Edwin's done his since he was ten!

Lucas They look okay. Cleaning shoes is another con. But Edwin's a different boy. (*Pause.*)
I've never cleaned them.

Reb I have.

Lucas No. Mum. You haven't.

Reb Lucas. I have.

Lucas No.

Reb Yes.

He grabs her fiercely by the jaw.

Lucas No. Rebecca. Not these boots. These ones you told me to do myself.

Reb Whatever you say.

Lucas Whatever you say. What kind of reply is that?

A moment.

Did you really clean them?

Reb Why do you s'pose they look okay?

Lucas How many times have I told you not to interfere with my stuff?

Silence.

Reb I've spoilt you rotten.

Lucas Not rotten enough.

Reb I wish someone would spoil me that much.

Lucas How about me?

Reb You! Five minutes. That's your limit.

Lucas You never give me a chance. (*Pause.*)
Let's be friends. Kiss and make up.

*He gets up and stands in front of her. Embraces her.
Gently. She pats him on the back. Rests her hands
lightly on his shoulders in an unconscious gesture.
Ritualised, intimate and familiar. He doesn't move.*

Reb Okay, boy. I'm exhausted.

*Still Lucas doesn't move. Slowly runs his arm down
her back and pulls her in against him. She pushes him
away.*

Grow up, Lucas!

Lucas You really piss me off. (*Pause.*) The way you talk
on the telephone.

Reb Don't listen.

Lucas Going on and on to your friends. Giggling in that low voice. Recipes and men and children, and feminism and books and movies and art galleries. And you don't care who hears you. All things to all men, aren't you? Always trying to do the right thing.

Reb Not always, Lucas. Not always.

Lucas Be a great cook. Have a right-on job. Make beautiful pots. Look at them. They're useless. Study. Improve yourself. Be a good wife. You're so boring.

Reb And you're so abusive.

Lucas Why don't you go out and have some fun?

Reb Let me guess. You didn't get the job?

Lucas Yeah. Naturally I got the job. It's in your gift isn't it. Some geezer you know. You talk to him and of course it's landing in my lap nice and easy, isn't it? Because *you* can work miracles. Get the fuck out of my life, Mum. Obviously I didn't get the job. Would I even be here if I'd done?

Reb Swearing won't help.

Lucas Fucking bastard stupid git. Fucking bastard stupid git. Fucking bastard . . .

Reb Okay. Okay. So what went wrong?

Lucas What went wrong? You don't know what it's like out there. You sit in here like a big grey spider on its web. Pouncing on people when they come in and gobbling them up as if they were flies. And you're never satisfied. You always want more. More flies. More flies.

Reb Oh. So it's my fault you didn't get the job?

Lucas You've ripped off my wings.

Reb That's rich. So it's back to the gym is it now? And the high point of your day when you get to blow dry your pubes with a hair dryer? Think you're something special! They only let you in free because you're young and good-looking and you're prepared to rub down some fat old man with a Porsche in your shorts. What kind of sordid sub-culture is that?

Lucas You think you know everything.

Reb Everything you need to know. That's what mothers are for.

Lucas You didn't know your husband was unfaithful.

A very slight pause.

Reb Of course I know that. Why would you know that but not I?

Lucas He really gets off on other women.

Reb You talk about it?

Lucas I'm a witness.

Reb That's most unfortunate.

Lucas All the time, baby. I remember standing once in my pyjamas and watching with my lasso wishing I could loop it round his neck and haul him off her.

Reb I knew about that. We have a very strong marriage. I always put it first you know. Being a housewife. The maintenance of the spider's web you might say.

Lucas Are you very upset?

Reb Yes. Just a touch. You don't appear for days and don't tell me where you are. You come in like a burglar and a murderer. Not to lay a huge box of black chocolates at my feet. To take money from me. I would give it to you freely. To have a laugh at my expense. And drink a few beers. That's not so original. You don't want a job. You show me up all the time.

Lucas I love you.

Reb So tell me about love.

Lucas Come here.

Reb I can't bear the sight of you . . .

Lucas C'mon. Let me give you a cuddle. I'm sorry. Dad's a bastard.

He takes her gently in his arms. Attentive. Filial. Comforting. But then starts to caress her. He kisses her. Openly desirous.

Sorry, Mum. Sorry.

She is transfixed with horror. Ashamed he grabs her and shakes her.

Lucas React. Why don't you? Why don't you ever wear a skirt and high heels and go out dancing and have a good time? Kiss me.

He kisses her again.

You used to kiss me all the time.

Starts to cry.

I said I'm sorry. (*Pause.*) But that's love for you.

Reb No. There's . . . Love of mankind. Love and care. And art. And. Just little things you're fond of, you know, like light coming though coloured glass . . .

Lucas This is all there is. (*Pause.*)

'My mother made me a homosexual. If I buy her the wool will she make me one too?' (*Pause.*) My mother made me love her. If I love her back will she love me too?

Reb I've done nothing but love you since the day you were born.

Lucas No. No you haven't.

Reb Oh, God. Give me some champagne.

Lucas Shall we sit down.

She sits.

Relax.

She doesn't.

Reb Don't wave that blessed knife at me.

He sticks the knife into the table. She shifts further back.

Oh. My table.

Tries to relax.

Lucas That's better. (*Pause.*)

He gets another glass. Refills hers and one for himself.

Now sit further back on the table and put one leg up like that and hold it with your arm, like you were sitting chatting with a friend. Put your head back, like that, for a moment –

Let your leg fall open . . .

A moment.

He goes to arrange her legs. She starts back and as she does she knocks the ice-cream maker off the edge of the table. Semi-set raspberry ice-cream pours out onto the floor. He begins to laugh.

Lucas Now I'm really in the shit. She's not best pleased with me now.

Reb begins to weep. Lucas lies down on the floor and starts to lick the ice-cream up.

Lucas You're right. I do like your raspberry ice-cream.

He scoops some up in his hands and offers it to her. She declines.

Lucas All the more for me. Listen, Mum. You never listen to me. I think you are so beautiful. When I was little I used to tell myself I was going to marry you when I grow up. Ed and me. We used to fight about who was going to get you. I always thought it would be me.

Reb Please I have to go to bed now.

Lucas Take me with you.

Reb I'm desperately tired.

Lucas Don't you find me attractive?

Reb You're sick.

Lucas I've thought about it such a lot. Not exactly planning. Letting the idea flow through my mind till I can't leave you alone any longer. I adore you. I worship you. No other woman is a patch on you. (*Pause.*) I love those shorts. Especially when you sit like that. What is the fabric called?

Reb Polyester. Viscose. I don't know.

Lucas I love the way your leg looks in them. The inside of your thigh falling away from the muscle and the bone. The way the dirt runs into the sweat under your arm when you're working in the garden. I love the way you dress for me.

Reb I dress for myself.

Lucas Bullshit. You dress for me.

Reb Lucas. I dressed like this before you were born.

Lucas But now it's all for me.

Reb You're drunk.

Lucas You make me high.

Reb You'll forget all this in the morning.

Lucas I really fancy you.

Reb Look, I'm sorry. There's been some misunderstanding. This . . . sexual feeling. I reserve that for your father.

Lucas No you don't.

Reb Oh, Lucas. Mind your own business.

Lucas You don't do it very often.

Reb How would you know?

Lucas I never hear cries of pleasure. Or laughter from your room. You don't wear little lacy bits of underwear.

Reb We've been married for twenty years!

Lucas If you were my wife it wouldn't be like that.

Reb When you've been married for twenty years you'll have other things on your mind.

Lucas We're the perfect couple. You're at the height of your sexual powers. But you're not getting enough of it. I'm young. I have a lovely strong body which will last you all you want. (*Pause.*) I've been reading up on it.

Reb Pornographic magazines.

Lucas It doesn't matter. I know what I'm doing for once in my life.

A moment.

22

Lucas Your husband is a liar and a cheat. No one loves you. But me. No one but me wants to run his hand on the inside of your thigh and watch it shiver. But you want to shiver. Everyone wants someone to make them shiver. I can do that for you. Watch me do it. (*Pause.*) Show me how to do it. You taught me to tie shoelaces. You can do this. Tying shoelaces was much harder. (*Pause.*) Please Mum. I'm so nervous. I'm trembling with excitement and happiness. (*He ticks off a kind of checklist.*) No need for contraceptives. No sexually transmitted disease. We can experiment safely. We've got lots of time. (*Pause.*)
I'm dying to get back up there. Back up that great liner and flood that throbbing engine room.

Reb Help me. Someone. Help me.

Lucas Mum. I'm here.

Reb Edwin! Save me, Edwin!

Lucas He's staying at Louis' tonight.

Reb Help me! Help me!

Lucas Help *me*, Mum. Help *me*. I've never done this before.

Reb What?

Lucas I mean . . . At all.

Reb Oh, God.

Lucas I've been saving myself for you.

Reb Oh, Nick! Nick! (*Pause.*)

Lucas Hold the knife for me, will you? I tell you Mum I want this so much I would kill you for it.

Reb I'm your mother!

Lucas   I know. Isn't it wonderful?

He puts his hand on the inside of her thigh.

Did you see it shiver? Oh, my love. My lovely mother.

Scene Two

*The same. The next morning. Dawn. From the garden
the vibrant sounds of the dawn chorus.*

*Remains of raspberry ice-cream congealed on floor. Ice-
cream maker lies where it was.*

*Lucas creeps out from the direction of the bedroom.
Dressed in jeans, white tee-shirt, check shirt over. Pulling
on boots. Stops. Does up bootlaces, laboriously. Buttons
shirt. Gets cap from hook. Puts it on.*

*Slowly assembles fishing gear. Takes out bait from fridge.
Gets basket, umbrella, coat ready.*

*Gets all his stuff ready and stands, festooned with fishing
equipment.*

Lucas You motherfucker.

*Stands. Checks jeans. Puts his hand in his pocket and
takes out a ball of crushed material. It is his mother's
shorts.*

*He quickly puts them over the back of a chair and
turns away to leave.*

*The shorts fall off. He picks them up and hangs them
up again. They fall again.*

*He tries a third time. By now rather nervous. They fall
again.*

Lucas thoroughly disconcerted. He looks at them for a

moment. Leaves them and hurries out through the French doors.

A long moment.

Reb appears dressed as before, but missing her shorts. She seems cowed, embarrassed, without them. She moves carefully.

She looks for her shorts. Finds them and tries to put them on. She stumbles. She cannot get them on. Finally she has to sit on the floor and struggle into them.

A moment. She stands up again. Goes over to the sink and gets a drink of water. Stands looking around the room. She sees the champagne bottle and the ice-cream on the floor. Takes the bottle. Goes and stands in the ice-cream, watching it mush between her toes. Drinks from the bottle. Looks out at garden. Slowly stands. Abandons bottle and goes out French doors.

Time passes: morning.

Reb comes in from the garden with a wheelbarrow full of soil. She tips it up and empties the soil onto the ice-cream. She mixes the soil into the ice-cream with a spade, as if she were mixing cement.

Time passes: midday.

Reb polishing some glasses with a cloth, listening to a cheery radio programme, aimed at women. Without a pause she moves from polishing the glasses to polishing the leaves of some indoor plant.

Time passes: afternoon.

Reb stands studying the pots on the shelf and the African artefacts. They seem to puzzle her.

She goes and sits on the table. She looks down at her body. Lies down on the table.

During this scene Reb gets progressively dirtier as her kitchen gets cleaner.

Time passes. The sound of a floor being scrubbed.

Scene Three

*The same. Early evening. The kitchen is spotless. But
there is a stain on the floor.*

*Dory enters from the garden carrying a bottle of
champagne and a large oil painting.*

*Dressed predominantly in black; tee-shirt, cycling shorts,
and a small black frilly skirt like a ballet tutu. Dainty little
high-heeled boots with frilly socks.*

*Pinned to her left breast a large bunch of milliners'
flowers. Sunglasses.*

Dory   Yoo-hoo! Where are you birthday girl?

Silence.

*Dory puts the champagne in the fridge and displays the
painting prominently. The subject is a nude woman
bathing herself and a baby in a tiled room. The woman
has only one breast. But it is a painting with lots of life
and colour.*

*She stands for a bit and then starts to snoop around, at
the food, and other things she sees. Takes note of the
stain on the floor. Looks at the pottery bowls. Wipes
her finger along a shelf. No dust.*

Fucking hell!

*She sits quietly in a shadowy corner of the room, Lights
a cigarette. Smokes. Studies her painting. Waits.*

*A crashing sound outside in the garden. Suddenly a
skateboard is projected over the step into the room.*

Ridden by Edwin. It zips through the kitchen and crashes into the wall. A small piece of plaster falls down from the ceiling.

Edwin wears long, baggy shorts, a huge tee-shirt, sun-glasses with the glasses turned round to the nape of his neck, a rucksack and two cans of coke sticking out from his sides, held in position by his two elbows. In one hand he carries a billiard cue.

He puts the billiard cue away in a corner of the room. At odd moments, especially when nervous, Edwin picks up the cue and mocks at taking the odd shot. When he puts it down Reb inevitably tidies it away to the corner where Lucas's fishing equipment is kept.

He smiles. With a great flourish he catches the two coke cans, puts them down, takes out from the rucksack a chocolate cake in a box, a card, and a bunch of flowers. He arranges them on the table.

Goes over and looks at the wall where the skateboard crashed. Kicks away the little pile of plaster dust from the ceiling so it doesn't show.

Turns suddenly, startled. Sees Dory.

Edwin   Hi. Dory.

Dory   Hi. Sweetheart.

Edwin   Mum's birthday. Sorry. Only two cokes. Mum and me. Didn't know you were here. Where's Mum? Dad? Lucas?

Dory shakes her head.

Edwin   This is a no smoking house.

Dory   I know. It's too perfect.

She continues to smoke.

Dory Nick back from his travels?

Edwin Doesn't look like it.

Dory Explain.

Edwin It's noisier. When he's here. You know. The phone . . .

A moment.

You see this plaster dust.

Dory What dust? Can you see any dust?

Edwin Oh. Okay. Yeah. Thanks.

Dory shows him the painting.

Dory I brought her this. What do you think?

Edwin studies it seriously.

Edwin A one-breasted woman. She's only got one nipple.

Dory She was unlucky.

Edwin I guess one is enough.

Dory To get her into trouble. Yeah.

Edwin Cool.

A moment.

Dory Make a circle with your fingers round my wrist.

Edwin No. What for?

Dory Go on.

He does.

Edwin There.

Dory Thin isn't it?

Edwin Is that what you want?

Dory No. Not any more. No. (*Pause.*) I can still jive.

Edwin That's good.

Dory Want me to show you?

Edwin No thanks.

Dory Do you like girls?

Edwin They're okay.

Dory Do you have a girl?

Edwin shakes his head.

What about that girl, that Hannah-the-Spannah girl?

Edwin She's not a girl.

Dory Oh.

Edwin She's a friend.

Dory So what about a hug? For me.

Edwin No way.

Dory I'm not a girl either.

Edwin I don't hug female people ever.

Dory I used to change your nappy.

Edwin That's your problem.

Dory laughs. Lights up again.

Edwin Please don't have another cigarette.

Dory stops. Looks at him. Puts the cigarette out.

Dory Where is she, Edwin?

A hissing sound from the garden.

Reb   (*off*) Edwin? Edwin?

Edwin   Where the hell are you?

Reb   (*off*) Tree house. Can't get down.

Edwin   What do you mean – can't get down?

Reb   (*off*) I got up. I can't get down.

Edwin   What goes up must come down. Gravity, Mum.

Reb   (*off*) Please.

Edwin   What are you doing up there?

Reb   (*off*) Cleaning.

Edwin   Cleaning?

Reb   (*off*) Yes.

Dory   Did she say cleaning?

Edwin   Yes.

Dory   In a tree house?

Reb   (*off*) Get me down, Edwin.

Edwin   Just turn round and come down backwards.

Reb   (*off*) I can't. I've got this airgun.

Dory   You're not still shooting birds, are you?

Edwin   Come on, Mum. You can do it.

Dory   She takes this cleaning stuff very seriously. (*Indicates kitchen.*) What does she do to it? Lick it clean?

Edwin   Dory –

Dory   I know. You love her. She's your mum. Have some champagne.

Edwin   Wait up. Mum –

Dory   This'll do it. Watch.

Reb   (*off*) No. Oh no. No. No.

Sound of scuffling and slithering.

Dory   She's down!

She opens the champagne.

Lucas appears carrying Reb.

Reb is wearing a silk outfit, Oriental in style; full trousers gathered into her ankles, a long tunic top buttoned to the neck and with long sleeves. Pretty sandals, jewellery and make up. Vivid, but not bright colours. She cradles an old airgun.

Lucas wears waders and has other fishing gear festooned about him. He carries a rod. As well as his mother.

Throughout this scene he, like Edwin, picks up and 'plays' with his fishing rod. Whenever he puts it down Reb puts it away again.

Reb   I slipped –

Lucas stands. Reb seems to crouch in his arms.

Dory   What a strong chap! That has to be an old woman's dream. Look. He's breathing as quiet as a mouse. Let's have a go. Edwin?

Dory makes as if to leap into his arms.

He grimaces.

Reb   I was waiting for Nick.

Silence.

Dory   Do you remember that holiday in France – it must have been about seven years ago when we camped under a

33

plum tree and asked the farmer if we could gather the windfalls and he said it was okay as long as we didn't 'exciter la chute' – excite their fall? Remember boys?

Edwin   Put her down. Lukie. Let her go.

Lucas holds his hands out and Reb slides very slowly out of his arms.

Dory   How fantastic youth is.

Lucas   That why you dress like a Barbie Doll?

Edwin   Little frilly skirts. I thought you liked it. Said you wished Mum would –

Lucas throws a punch at Edwin who ducks and sprints from the room.

Silence.

Dory   The doors were open, Reb.

Lucas helps himself to a glass of champagne. Goes and turns the television on, lies on the sofa to watch it. Still wearing his waders.

Dory   Nice boy, Lucas. Never smiles.

Lucas   Never smile at a crocodile.

Reb   I've got this airgun. But it's all rusted over.

Dory   Put it down, Reb. Put it a long way away.

Reb takes the gun and puts it in the sink.

Reb   I'll wash it later.

Dory makes to hug Reb, but Reb recoils.

Dory   You in purdah or something?

They stare at each other. At each other's clothes.

Reb looks down at her own clothes.

34

Reb I want to look old.

Dory Sweetie. Not *that* old!

Reb reaches out and touches the bunch of flowers on Dory's tee-shirt. She pats them gently. Smiles.

Dory Silly, aren't they?

Reb It's because you're blonde.

Dory Good decision. That. To be blonde.

Reb You were, weren't you?

Dory No.

Reb A real blonde?

Dory No.

Reb At college?

Dory Never.

Reb Never?

Dory No.

Reb I thought you were.

A moment.

Don't flirt with my sons.

Dory I'll flirt with whoever I like.

Reb They're only boys.

Dory They're over sixteen, aren't they? Oh calm down. It's not *Just William* now you know.

Reb Nick's coming back tonight. (*Pause.*)
I don't like all these African things he imports. It's like coffin chasing.

Dory Well. (*Pause.*)

Dory Happy Birthday! (*Toasting her.*) To maturity! Toler-
ance and understanding! And forgiveness! God. Don't cry.
I can't stand emotion. In humans. (*Pause.*) Here. Have
this.

She shows the painting to Reb.

Reb studies it.

Reb It doesn't look like me!

Dory It's meant to be me!

A moment.

Dory Yeah. Well. You don't have to have it.

Reb I want it.

Dory All these women walking around with only one
breast. I thought it must irk them looking at paintings and
bra adverts, you know. Two perfect titties. So I just gave
her one.

Reb You've started painting again.

Dory I saw Roy.

Reb Roy?

Dory He invited us for tea. At the Ritz. I haven't seen
him in the flesh for years. I sat there with my tea cup and
watched him falling in love with his own daughters.
(*Pause.*) He wrote them each a large cheque. Then
afterwards sent round two of his paintings. I wish he'd
bloody sent the money to insure them. (*Pause.*)

He's trying to avoid death duties. You know how the
really rich are such arseholes. Never bothered to see them.
Never gave me a sou. They don't care if he lives or dies.
Why should they?

A moment.

Dory I haven't been able to sleep since then. This is what I've been doing instead.

Silence.

Talk to me, Reb. It's your birthday.

Reb It's a wonderful painting.

Dory And what about you? Your pottery. You were good.

Reb shrugs.

Dory And what you do now is better? That women's refuge? Just other people's old crap. Got enough of your own, haven't you? I'd go back to your pots.

Reb I tell you that's all finished!

Dory No. It's here now. This place is beautiful, Reb. (*Her gesture takes in the kitchen, the garden, the meal.*) This is what you pour it into now.

Reb Thank you.

Dory What's this doing here? (*Indicates computer.*)

Reb I hate it.

Dory Get rid of it.

Reb It can't be moved. Sounds silly, doesn't it? But Lucas says without it in here he feels overpowered. You know like drenching the room with perfume or something.

Silence.

Dory tries to shift the computer. Reb stops her.

Reb Please don't.

Dory Shit Reb. Look at him.

Reb wraps herself around the computer to stop Dory moving it.

Lucas gets up slowly and stands staring at Dory.

Dory Have you two gone completely crazy?

Reb The French doors. I leave them open for the boys. To come and go as they please. When they were small they used to run in and out with their trophies. Pebbles and snails and nuts from the trees.

Silence.

Edwin comes in. A ghetto blaster on his shoulder. Playing hip-hop music:

'I come home from school. Hug me mum. Kiss me sister. Punch me brother. I go to me room to watch some teevee. Hhhrrr.

'Do my ears deceive me? No. Love's going to get you. Hhhrrr. Hhhrrr. Love's going to get you . . . '

Edwin See, Dory. Hug me mother. That's all. Not her friend.

Dory I get it.

Edwin When's Dad home?

Reb Any minute.

Edwin goes out with his ghetto blaster.

Lucas You doing dirty pictures now Dory?

Dory And butter wouldn't melt in your mouth.

Lucas What's for supper?

Dory It's your mother's birthday.

Lucas So?

Dory Well.

Lucas We're still having supper, aren't we?

Dory She's making something special tonight.

Lucas I don't like that stuff.

Dory That's easy. Don't come.

Lucas Mum!

Reb I'll do him something else.

Dory No you won't.

Lucas When? I'm starving. I haven't eaten all day.

Dory Catch any fish?

Lucas Yeah.

Dory Eat them.

Lucas I don't eat fish.

Dory You treat this place like a saloon.

Lucas gobs some spit or gum right across the room into a beautiful hand-painted bowl on a shelf.

As it lands in the bowl Edwin appears, with ghetto blaster still going, and tips up the bowl so they can see. He grins.

Lucas Did you see that?

Dory That's one of your mother's. It's valuable.

Lucas Reckon I could get something for it?

Edwin sits on one end of the sofa. The effect is to create a clash of sounds between the t.v. and the tape deck. Neither boy modifies their volume. Edwin stares for a few moments at the telly. Lucas listens to the music.

Lucas It's crap.

Edwin Yeah. It is. What are you watching it for?

Lucas This isn't crap! That's crap!

Edwin Get cool man. You're outta date. (*Pause.*) Have you seen my money? I had a load of money saved up for Mum's birthday –

Lucas No.

Edwin I could have sworn it was in my fish tank.

  A moment.

Are you absolutely certain, Lukie?

Lucas I'm completely skint too. Mum. I'm starving.

Dory You lazy slob.

  Edwin goes out.

Lucas Mum. Get rid of her, will you? This is a family occasion.

Dory Why don't you get yourself a girlfriend?

Lucas Why should I?

Dory Aren't you interested in sex?

Lucas I love my mum.

Dory What's all the hunky body bit for? It isn't boys.

Lucas Well, Dory if you want to know. I have a secret life. It involves older women. And for the woman of my dreams I want to make myself so beautiful and so strong that she'll never need to look at another man.

Dory It's the telly. What's that programme?

Lucas I get bored just hanging around at home doing nothing. I like to have a set of fitness goals to keep to.

(*He goes up to Dory and flexes his muscles.*) What do you think? No. Go on. Touch it. (*She doesn't.*) Scared to, aren't you? Case you faint. (*Takes off shirt and tee-shirt. Drapes the shirt over Dory's painting, balls the tee-shirt in his hand.*) Tell me Dory. How do you feel about body hair? How do you rate it on a scale one to ten? (*Parades bare torso around.*) What about that then? You're sick, Dory. You're bulimic, you are.

Dory   You disgust me.

Lucas   I'd have you if I saw you on the street.

Dory   So I never walk my dog this way.

Lucas   Have you got a dog, Dory?

Dory   Not many. (*Pause.*)

Lucas   Mum. Please. I'm really hungry. How about chicken, mashed potatoes and French beans. Before Dad gets back.

Dory   You're not going to do it, Reb.

Lucas   She will when you've gone.

Reb   He doesn't like elaborate meals.

Dory   Well fuck him Reb! Just this once!

Lucas starts to laugh.

Dory   I'd kill him if he treated me like that. Can't he get a girl?

Silence.

I need a fag.

She lights up.

They stare at her.

She goes out into the garden.

Reb and Lucas stand staring at each other. First one. Then the other make a move toward each other. But cannot proceed.

He gives her a package.

Lucas   I'm sorry.

Silence.

I'm sorry.

Silence.

I never told anyone. I never told Edwin.

Reb makes a gesture.

This . . . I can't be the only one. It must happen all the time.

Reb starts to laugh.

I'm okay. Are you okay?

Silence.

Don't tell Dad. Please. If I'm not here you won't need to think about it. It's. It's just. Nothing happened. (*Pause.*) Look I blow you a kiss. Dad will look after you. And you will look after Ed. It'll be okay. I'll be okay. Say you're okay now. Say you're okay now.

Silence.

Slowly, painfully, Reb takes a small folded note from her sleeve. She passes it with great difficulty to Lucas.

Lucas opens it and reads it aloud.

'Go to Aunt Judith's after dinner. I'll send you some money there. Farewell. My precious.'

Lucas turns the note over.

'I love you.' (*Pause.*) 'I love you.'

A moment.

Is that it? Is that it?

Edwin comes in.

Edwin Ah ha! Presents! Show us what it is. What did he get you, Mum?

He picks up his own birthday offerings, the cake and flowers and the two cans of coke and waits to give them to her.

Slowly Reb opens the package Lucas gave her. She holds up a set of lacy, silk, grey underwear. Expensive.

Wow!

He looks at his own presents.

Hold it up again, Mum. (*To Lucas.*) You said you didn't have any money! You took my money, didn't you? You took my money! And look what you bought her! And left me with almost nothing. This was all I could afford.

Reb embraces Edwin tenderly, awkwardly. They stand facing each other for a moment. Reb puts her hands up and straightens his collar. Her hands rest lightly on his shoulders. A moment.

Reb Thank you, my love.

Edwin (*crying*) Try it on, Mum. The underwear. It's neat. I really gave you that present. It's really from both of us. You like it don't you?

Dory comes in from the garden.

Dory Try them on, Reb.

Silence.

43

Dory   Why grey?

Lucas   Grey because her hair is grey. Grey because she cries a lot. Grey because she's fifty and beautiful and it suits her olivey skin.

Dory   Boy. Well. Part of you is functioning okay.

Edwin   He bought it with my money! My money in the fish tank!

Dory   (*to Lucas*) You bought your mother an expensive birthday present with money you'd just nicked from your baby brother?

Reb   (*to Dory*) I thought you'd gone.

Edwin   You make Mum cry. You're always –

Lucas   Shut it!

Edwin grabs the lingerie from Reb and goes off with it. Lucas tries to trip him up. He nearly succeeds. Edwin stumbles but escapes. Lucas after him.

Dory   He's a good kid. I've always liked him. (*Pause.*) He could use some attention. If you weren't so bloody besotted with that monster –

Reb   Shut up!

Dory   Lucas.

Reb slaps Dory.

Christ!

Reb   I beg your pardon.

Dory   Always was. Ever since he was a baby.

A moment.

Reb   The children used to like each other.

44

Dory   No. They didn't. I had to bribe them to go on those holidays with you. It was murder. They hated him. And you. Pandering to his every whim. Tense as hell. Occasionally letting fly with an almighty whack.

Reb   But you came anyway.

Dory   I was on my own. With two small children. (*Pause.*) We did our bit. We played with Edwin. (*Pause.*) And Nick and I would go off sometimes and knock back a few stiff drinks and play cards. It was fun. Remember?

Reb   I was probably in bed.

Dory   Yes. He slept inside your nightie till he was three didn't he? (*Pause.*) Well. That's Nick's story.

Reb   He had trouble getting off to sleep.

Dory   All you had to do was say 'no'.

Reb   I said 'no' a million times.

Dory   And never meant it once.

Reb   You've been lucky with the girls.

Dory   It wasn't luck.

Reb   I wish I'd had a girl.

Dory   You're just a lousy mother.

   Silence.

Reb   You never said anything.

Dory   Not my job.

Reb   Out of friendship?

Dory   Friendship never made anything easier.

Nick appears at the French doors. He wears a very fashionable, casual suit, and has several pieces of luggage with him.

At the same time Edwin and Lucas appear from another room. They don't immediately see Nick.

Edwin is wearing Reb's shorts and tee-shirt. Lucas grabs a glass of champagne as he follows.

Lucas You look quite like Mum.

They see Nick. Edwin immediately starts prancing round the room, imitating Reb's gestures and manner.

Lucas starts to laugh hysterically.

Edwin *(to Nick)* Hello, darling. Lovely to see you after all this time. Have you had a great trip? I missed you so much.

He gives Nick a glass of champagne and a peck on the cheek.

Lucas leaves the room.

Mm. You smell good. Manly. Shall I get you your slippers? Or would you like to go straight to bed for a bit of nookie?

He quickly sheds the shorts and tee-shirt and reveals himself in the new grey lingerie, the bra stuffed etc. He scampers about the room, 'teasing' his father.

Reb, Nick and Dory stand watching.

A moment.

Edwin beats a hasty retreat.

Nick What were those gorgeous, lacy things he had on?

Dory Reb's.

Nick Reb?

Dory A birthday present.

Nick From you?

Dory Lucas.

Nick What?

Dory Yes.

Nick Where's he get the money from? He didn't get the job did he? (*No answer.*) He's got good taste. I'll say that for him. They must suit you.

Dory Edwin doesn't look bad.

They laugh.

Nick turns to Reb. Gives her another bottle of champagne, with a bow on it, flowers, chocolates, etc. He kisses her several times on the top of her head.

Nick Happy birthday dearest Reb! And Dory! My number one and two favourite women.

He gives Dory a perfunctory embrace.

Nick What are you doing here?

Dory Reb's fiftieth, of course.

A moment.

Dory And. I want you to sell some paintings.

Nick Not Roy's I hope.

Dory Roy's belong to the girls.

Nick How is the old bastard?

Dory Fuck knows.

Nick Very, very wealthy at the last count.

Dory Nick! Paintings of mine.

Nick What will the day bring next?

Dory Be serious.

Nick I'll try.

Dory takes Lucas's shirt off the painting and hurls it across the room.

Nick You look great, Dory. Thin. Been working out?

Reb goes out.

Nick studies the painting for a long time.

Nick Wow! It's okay. Best thing you've ever done.

Dory I know.

Nick You're not desperate.

Dory I want to make some money. For the first time. The only time in my life. I want to give the girls some money. Money from me.

Nick Are there more?

Dory About seven. The best is –

Nick This disabled woman metaphor is good. Topical. And its sincere too. It's really got something. She seems so angry. Very powerful. I think I can sell them. Bring them to the gallery next week.

Dory You can't come –

Nick No.

Dory It's people like you, Nick, helped me to get angry.

Nick What have you got to be angry about? More than the rest of us? (*Pause.*) You don't need to sell paintings.

Reb reappears. She's wearing Edwin's shorts and tee-shirt, and sunglasses. She carries the skateboard. She stands unnoticed.

Her speech a duet with Dory's.

Reb I think I've let myself go. (*Pause.*) Years ago. I don't remember the years. I promised Edwin I'd have a go on this. So here I am. I'm just going out on the pavement to see what I can do with it. I've watched him enough. I've picked him up from the ground enough. Bloody but unbowed. I should have learnt something by now. I should.

Dory In the future I want someone to look at that and know that that was what I did. I was a mother most of all, and I'm proud of it, but I did work too. Mostly I taught and I kept my girls going and now they're launched on their lives. They're lovely children. (*Pause.*) He didn't see them for fifteen years. And now he's in the mood to buy them back. They're so beautiful and charming. He likes all that. And I won't be able to stop him. And he'll ply them with money and they'll be rich and famous and successful.

Reb goes out through the garden.

Nick He's not evil.

Dory You don't understand. I thought you would.

Nick He *is* their father.

Dory No. You are.

Nick I'm not.

Dory How do you know?

Nick Well . . .

Dory Well?

Nick Don't fuck me up too, Dory.

Dory You could be. Spiritually. I was thinking about you.

Nick They look like him.

Dory You mended my toaster. You helped them do their homework.

Nick I didn't mend your toaster.

Dory Didn't you? I feel sure it was you. Who did then?

Nick There were plenty of others.

Dory No. Nowhere near my toaster.

Nick It wasn't me, Dory. I leave all that sort of thing to Reb.

Dory Who is it Nick? The other. For you now?

Nick What makes you think that?

Dory You've changed, Nick. You've forgotten. It was you who mended the toaster.

An American football curves through the air and Nick reaches out to catch it.

Edwin (*off*) Is Mum upset?

Nick throws the ball off. Edwin catches as he enters.

Dory She's gone skateboarding.

Edwin What? My skateboard? She'll break it!

Nick I got that tape you wanted –

Edwin Later, Dad. Later.

Edwin goes into the garden.

Nick goes back to the painting. He studies it with pleasure.

Dory   Not that one. That painting's not for sale.

Nick   For me?

Dory   It's Reb's.

Nick   Reb?

Dory   Yes.

Nick   Oh.

He stares at the painting. Then at Dory.

You've got cancer. You've had a breast removed.

Dory   How do I look?

Nick stares at the flowers on her tee-shirt. Tries to take her in his arms. Dory steps back.

No. Don't touch me. I'm a survivor.

A moment.

Nick   What's going on? Where's the boy?

Dory   Horrible man.

Nick   He hates you.

Dory   Are you blind? He's crazy about me.

Nick   I dream about him –

Dory   I know.

Nick   Do you ever think he . . . remembers?

Dory   Maybe.

Nick   That's unconscionable.

Dory   Yes.

Nick   Well then we're all finished.

A moment.

Dory   Magic Maestro. Give us some of your legendary magic.

Reb and Edwin come in through the garden. Reb's knees bleeding. Edwin carrying the skateboard.

Reb   I grazed my knees.

Edwin   That's what the knee-pads are for.

Reb   *You* don't wear them.

Nick   Ah, but he's young and lithe.

Reb   So?

Nick   So nothing. You've never been very agile. You've said it yourself often enough.

Reb   So?

Nick   Grow up, Reb.

Reb   Grow up yourself.

Edwin   She's not very good on ladders either.

Dory   How many times in your life will you have to climb in and out of a tree house, for Chrissake?

Edwin   Depends if you want to play in there.

Nick   Or if you're trying to build it.

Reb   Excuse me. I'm here. I make this house look like this. I make this food look like this. I make this garden look like this. If I weren't here all of this would disappear. And so would you.

Nick   Look. I've brought you a beautiful birthday present.

Nick hands Reb a large package. Roughly but securely tied up in brown hessian. She starts to undo it but doesn't take all the wrapping off. Reveals an African carving – a sculpture of a head.

Reb I don't find this beautiful. I don't want any more of these things. Look at them. Glowering down at me. This isn't Africa. This is here. A much more temperate zone. It doesn't work. If you ask these pieces what they want I know what their answer would be. They want to go home. They don't like it here. I can't say that I blame them. I have tried to tell you. Just today. I explained . . .

Dory No. Reb. That was me. You told me.

Reb Honestly I have to tell you, Nick, that I just hate them and I can't go on . . . any . . . longer . . . with . . .

Lucas walks into the room. They all stare at him.

Lucas Mum's obviously distressed. She's very tired. She's been working flat out to make this dinner for all of us. I think what she's trying to say, Dad, if I've got this right, is that she feels these are like the Elgin Marbles. Which you've stolen. In a way. And Mum, this is Dad's work. You've got to respect it. He feels he's bringing this art to the attention of the rest of the world. He can't help it if he doesn't any longer understand your likes and dislikes.

They continue to stare at him.

Shall we have dinner now?

He opens a bottle of champagne and starts to fill glasses. They appear to concur with this advice. He takes a big swallow. Then –

Without warning a scream from Edwin. He charges at Lucas with his billiard cue. Pokes it into his chest and knocks him to the floor.

Edwin You slimey, scummy bitch of a bastard.

Lucas grabs the cue and wrestles with it. Edwin still holding the other end.

She's not allowed to love anyone but you.

Edwin, like a terrier attached to a stick being waved by its master, seems to fly about the room as Lucas shakes the cue. Eventually he flies off the end.

Lucas snaps the cue in half and throws it aside.

Lucas I could have hit him with this. I could have killed him. I didn't use it.

Silence.

Nick Get out of here, you great bully. You've always been a bully, Lucas.

Lucas gets up slowly.

Edwin shoves a shard of the broken cue into Lucas's eye.

Lucas screams and runs from the room.

Edwin He's been really hassling Mum. He never tells her when he's coming home. He's always drunk. He was rude to Dory. And he stole my money . . .

Edwin runs from the room.

Off. Sound of room being smashed up.

Nick He didn't manage to blind him anyway.

Reb What did you say?

Reb hurries off.

Nick That'll cost me . . . Fuck . . . I . . .

Dory Why don't you go?

Nick I don't want to be beaten to death with a dumb-bell. Besides what can I do? He's always preferred her to me.

Edwin (*off*) No. Mum. No. You're not going in there. I'll look after him.

Sound of struggle. Sound of face being slapped. Reb screams. A moment.

Reb comes in holding the side of her face. She stands looking at Nick and Dory. For a long time.

Dory lifts her foot and with the tip of her boot pushes the computer over.

Dory leaves through the garden.

Scene Four

The same. Later that night. The table set for four. Where only two have eaten. Reb and Nick sit alone at table in a kind of lonely silence. Reb still in Edwin's skateboarding gear. Nick in shirtsleeves.

Reb gets some rubber gloves which she draws on very slowly. She starts clearing up.

Nick We went on a long trip by river, stopping at each village. So the stuff I've got this time is quite new. I wish you could see it. It's such a wonderful landscape. And it's all there in the work. I don't suppose you'd like to have a look at the photos? (*Pause.*) No. Of course you don't want to look at the photos. After all you never want to look at the photos. Or hear about what I've been doing. (*Pause.*) You know I play this little game with myself. I ask myself every time whether Reb's going to try to make herself take an interest. And I always lose. Because I'm on your side. I'm on the side that thinks one day Reb is going to take an interest.

Silence.

Fuck it, Reb. It's what I do. It's my work. It's my life.

No response.

It pays for all this!

Reb shakes her head.

What? You think you pay for it?

Reb continues to shake her head.

Oh. Don't tell me about problems. I want to look forward.

Reb I've spent my life looking forward.

Nick Alright, Reb. You win.

Reb laughs.

Reb You buy new underwear every time you go away. I used to think it was just a kind of tropico-fastidiousness. I never go away. Only to my father's. To clean him up. And the house. I take my oldest clothes.

Nick So. Go on.

Silence.

Ask me why.

Reb I don't want to ask you why.

A moment.

Did it have to be Dory?

Silence.

Why?

Nick A sort of dreariness.

Reb The start of your marriage. I was dreary.

Nick You were solid.

Reb And Dory?

Silence.

Nick I didn't want to be a dealer. God. I wanted to paint.

Silence.

Nick   We were unhappy.

Reb   *I* was unhappy.

Nick   So we were all unhappy.

Long moment.

Reb   So it was Dory?

Nick   You didn't know? No one told you?

Reb   No. I didn't know. Silly me. And no one told me.

Nick   I thought you must have . . . The way you spoke . . .

Reb   Funny, isn't it? I would never have known that. Would never have dreamed it possible. (*Pause.*)

Tell me . . .

A moment.

Reb   Did we wait too long to have the children?

A moment.

Dory was my friend.

Nick   My friend too.

Reb   But you broke a rule.

Silence.

When Lucas was a tiny baby I used to walk him in the park. I liked the feeling that I was only going for him. No other purpose. I was aware of all the other women and all the other prams and pushchairs. The balls. The buckets and spades. Spare nappies. Drinks and little snacks. To passers-by they probably seemed very lucky, with an easy time ahead of them, nothing much to do and lots of time to sit and talk to other women. I was attracted by all of that. Then I didn't really do it. I sort of gave it up without even knowing what it was. I was trying to do some other things at the same time. And so I missed out. You have to know what you're doing to be able to do nothing.

A long moment.

Nick You left me. You left me for Lucas.

Reb I didn't mean to do that.

Nick It's what you did.

Reb goes up to Nick. Stands in front of him. With tiny movements she straightens his collar. Rests her hands lightly on his shoulders. A moment of relaxation for them both. Suddenly she cries out in pain.

Reb Oh, God!

Nick Are you ill?

She walks away from him.

Reb I tried to get back. Every day of my life I've been trying to get back to you.

Nick I thought you knew best. You were the mother.

Reb Edwin is alright.

Nick Yes.

Reb Why is Edwin alright? (*Pause.*) When I lie in bed and can't sleep and think Lucas wants to kill me and that I'm going crazy I say to God. If I've done wrong. If I've done it all wrong. If I don't know how to be a mother why is Edwin alright? And God says. Well, Edwin isn't yours. He's an angel. And I've sent him down to be with your family so you can see what's it like to raise a fine boy. So Edwin's just on loan. He's not really ours. Like a library book that we keep renewing. And God could take him back anytime. (*Pause.*) Lucas is your son, God says.

See if you can't do better. And every morning I get out of bed resolved. And by the end of breakfast every day I want to slit his throat. (*Pause.*) He gets down a bowl. And fills it with cornflakes.

Reb gets down a packet of cornflakes and as she speaks she goes through the movements she is describing. Nick transfixed.

Then fills it up with milk. He pours sugar all over it. He leaves the packet on the table. Spilt milk and the top scattered with sugar. The milk bottle. The sugar bowl. He goes off with his bowl, slopping, spilling. He eats. Maybe half. Then he puts it down somewhere. And leaves it there.

Reb stares at the mess she has made. She does not clear it up.

What have you been doing? During all these cornflakes where were you?

Nick   The shower? (*Pause.*) It was him or me. (*Pause.*) I think about other things. Things that don't give me pain.

Reb   Why don't you challenge him?

Nick   You fill his whole eye.

Reb   But why?

A moment.

Nick   Do you know what it feels like to have this handsome man who was once a boy holding my hand. Digging holes in the garden. Inviting me in to look for worms. We used to sit on riverbanks spitting cherry pips. To have this stranger living beside me in the house? Knocking on each other's door. Walking politely round each other when we meet in the hall. Exchanging pleasantries about fishing. *I* taught him to fish!

Reb We've done something wrong.

Nick Oh, Reb. In Africa the families –

Reb Shut up about Africa. (*Pause.*) I'm sick of talking about him. He's always here. Do you know that? Always, always here. Why doesn't he study? Why doesn't he work? Why doesn't he do anything? Tell me Nick. Why doesn't he have a girl?

Nick Are you serious?

Reb We'll have to find him a place.

Nick *He* has to find a place.

Reb He has no money.

Nick I'll give him money. For a month. Lodging and food. Then he's on his own.

Reb He won't be able to handle it.

Nick He'll have to.

Reb It's impossible to get a job.

Nick He'll have to do something.

Reb If he claims benefit they'll expect him to live with us.

Nick He's not coming back.

Reb We're in a loop. We've been down this road before.

Nick Not far enough. Go on. Reb. Just go on.

Reb We're throwing him out.

Nick It's time.

Reb I feel terrible.

Nick I feel good.

Reb You don't love him.

Nick I want him to love me.

Reb I can't do this if you're not here. Supposing he comes round. He will. He'll just come in and start watching television.

Nick There won't be a television.

Reb He'll bring it.

Nick We'll change the locks.

Reb He'll break the door.

Nick We move house. He won't know where we've gone.

Reb Oh, Christ. We're going mad.

Nick I've had enough.

Reb Will you talk to him.

Nick Tonight.

Reb I can't be involved.

Nick You must be here. He's got to see us united on this.

Reb Your son.

Nick Reb. I dread coming back here.

Reb Really.

Nick He comes in here at night banging around the place. Just when we're at peace. And we lie there scarcely daring to breathe. Then by the time he's thrown up and gone to bed it's too late and I know in the dark your face is a mask of pain. (*Pause.*) Are you surprised I make love to people when I'm away?

Reb What? A whole tribe?

A moment.

Nick I was going to go.

Reb Go where?

Nick Leave all this.

Reb When was that going to be?

Nick When Edwin finished school.

Reb Tell me about it.

Nick To move back to Africa. Work from there.

Reb Was I coming?

Nick No.

Reb What was I going to do?

Nick Whatever you want.

Reb stares at him.

She goes over to the half unwrapped African sculpture. She stands looking at it without touching it.

Reb Her hands have handled that head. Helped you choose. Is she African?

Nick Yes.

Reb A colleague?

Nick Yes.

Reb That must be nice.

Nick An archaeologist.

Reb Young?

Nick Yes.

Reb Very?

Nick Fairly.

Reb   Will it go on?

Nick   Depends on you.

Reb   Depends on me. Fuck you. Depends on you.
Why don't you go now. Tonight.

Nick   I want to stay now.

Reb   I want you to go. I have a lover too by the way.
That's why I'm tired. And irritable. I didn't get any sleep
last night.

Nick   Keep your voice down. The boys might hear.

Reb   Edwin's asleep. Lucas's gone.

Nick   He'll be back. Give him a few hours. (*Pause.*)
You're a lousy drunk. You're hallucinating. You just said
you'd been out all night making love with a . . . with
someone else.

Reb   I wasn't out. I was here. Cooking.

Nick   There.

Reb   With a lover. I don't even like champagne. No one
knows what I like to drink. Isn't that funny?

Nick   Stop messing about Reb. You mean a book?

Reb   Yeah I do love my books! No. I mean flesh. Human
flesh. Two hot, wet bodies sliding around each other. One
of them was mine. Get it? (*Pause.*)

Nick   Is that it?

Reb   That's it.

Nick   Was this a one off? Or . . .

Reb   A truly unforgettable experience. But once was
enough.

Nick Someone I know.

Reb Of course.

Nick I can't think of anyone . . .

Reb So hard to imagine?

Nick The milkman? A workman?

Reb That sort of thing.

Nick You must be desperate.

Reb That's what I think.

Nick Not Dory?

Reb Dory. Dory. Dory. My head's buzzing with Dory.
You think because I don't want you –

Nick Why don't you want me?

Reb Because I'm tired of getting it wrong.

A moment.

It's a feller alright. A gorgeous handsome young man.

A moment.

Nick Well, Reb.

Reb Well. Fancy me.

Nick You have to laugh.

Nick attempts to embrace her. She pushes him away.

Nick You took precautions. I trust.

Reb What a joke.

Nick That makes us even.

Reb No. Never.

Nick How's that?

Reb That was a big secret for a small child to hold.

Nick I don't understand.

Reb You and Dory. In bed. And a little boy alongside.

Nick He never saw her. I covered her up before he stepped into the room. Totally. Very fast. I covered her with the sheets.

Reb You fool.

Nick And you. Sweet lady.

Reb Listen to this stuff.

Nick Grabbing some young man. To pay me back.

Reb You polluted our lives.

Nick You exaggerate.

Reb What have we done?

Silence.

Nick We could start afresh.

Reb Start what, Nick?

Nick Now that it's all in the open. We could. I feel quite hopeful.

Reb We aren't an apple tree, Nick. Where we can just leave the old worm-eaten apples to rot on the ground, throw out some blossom in the spring, call over the bees, and make some lovely new apples next year. Is that how you'd like it to be? Let me tell you what you need to know. The tree is sick. The tree is dying. Those were our only apples.

A long moment.

I must tell you about my lover . . .

Nick   Only if you want to –

Edwin suddenly appears. Dressed in black. Rucksack on his back. Carrying his skateboard.

Where are you off to son? It's much too late.

Reb   Edwin. No. Don't take the skateboard. Please. Please don't. It'll be alright.

She falls to her knees in front of Edwin.

Please. Don't take it. Please.

Nick   It's okay. He doesn't like rows. I'll sort him out tomorrow.

Reb   Please God. Let me keep Edwin. Let him stay.

Edwin leaves through the garden.

Nick   Why not? Wouldn't you?

Reb goes and stands looking out at the garden. A long moment.

Reb   Lucas is my lover.

A moment.

Don't look at me please.

A moment.

I didn't chose him. He chose me. He caught me here alone. I didn't know what was coming. I called out for help but there was nobody here. Just him and me. He thinks it all makes sense. That we were made for each other. That he loves me. Like no one else ever has. Or can. And that I love him. And I'm the only one who ever will. He had a knife. He made me hold the knife. He wanted both hands free.

Nick   He gave you the knife.

Reb I know what you're saying. That I should have done something to hurt him. How could I? He was my son. My own flesh and blood.

Nick Oh, God.

Reb There was no God last night.

Nick I don't believe this.

Reb I don't believe it either.

Nick No one would believe us.

Reb He said you wouldn't believe me.

Nick You must have struggled.

Reb It wasn't like that.

Nick You should have struggled, Reb.

Reb That's what they all say. All the men to all the women.

Nick People think we're nice people. With a rather awkward son.

Reb Most of the time I seem to be alright. I go to the door to shake hands . . . That unimaginable gap between what we look like seen from out there and what's really going on here at home. It makes you wonder what's going on in all the other houses. (*Pause.*) He said he would tell you I had seduced him.

Nick suddenly grabs his head in pain and shouts.

Nick I'm going deaf!

Reb You've leapt over to the other side. And I've been left stuck inside with this. I don't seem to have an outside any more.

Nick Did he . . . ?

68

Reb Did he? Ah. Did he?

Nick Did he?

Reb Yes. He did.

Nick Did you . . . ?

Reb He kept saying it would be lovely. That I mustn't worry any more. That he would only do it if I wanted him to.

Nick So. Then.

Reb Where were you, Nick? Why weren't you here? Hold me in your arms. Now. Tell me you love me.

Nick holds his head in agony.

He took me by the hand – I held the knife in the other hand – or did he have his arm about my neck? I don't remember. He led me into the bathroom. He ran a bath and put me in it. Then he washed me. All the time talking gently, soothing, paying me compliments, touching, exploring, caressing. I remember thinking. If this is what people pay hundreds of pounds for when they go to those special bath places. Then it's probably money well spent. I kept pretending to myself that this was what I was doing. Paying for sex. Risqué. But nice. No real harm. If I could just hold onto that idea I could manage. My soul would survive. But then it was his voice. My own son. Over and over. How much he loved me. How much he wanted me. How much he hoped I would be able to relax and enjoy myself. That my frown – my famous frown – would wash away.

Nick Enough.

Reb No. Listen.

Nick Please, Reb. Please don't tell me about it.

Reb I have to tell someone.

A moment.

The drops of water on the blue and green tiles seemed very beautiful. Fresh and clean. And I remembered why we'd chosen them. All those years ago. He dried me in a big, white, soft towel I had never seen before. Then he took me and laid me on the bed and rubbed me all over with sweet smelling oils. He lit a candle. All the time asking if I was feeling any better. He said I needed cherishing.

Nick Don't I need cherishing too?

Reb He kept saying. You did all this for me. So many times when I was a kid. And now its your turn to have me do it for you. I felt like I was being laid out, getting ready to be dead. Was he just going to kill me? Smother me with something? I fell asleep. I must have slept for a few minutes. I felt peaceful and relieved. (*Pause.*) I thought I could handle it and that morning must soon be here. But then he was there beside me. He's showered and shaved and smells very young and brave. He says he belongs in me.

A long moment.

I remember when he was born. Such a long, long labour.

A long moment.

Crucifying, isn't it?

A long moment.

Nick This all happened here?

Reb Last night.

Nick I don't believe a word of it.

Reb I don't either. So that's okay.

70

Nick You realise you can't prove any of this.

Reb That's right.

Nick Either it was someone else. Or it wasn't Lucas.

Reb I must have dreamed it all.

Long silence. As if they have fallen asleep.

Nick Reb?

Reb Yes.

Nick Forgive me.

Reb Yes.

Nick Can I get you anything?

Reb Yes.

Nick A glass of water.

Reb Thank you.

Nick gets her a glass of water.

He looks out at the garden.

Nick I can see it's been pretty hot here. It doesn't show when I stand at these doors and look out. The garden is perfect. Lush and verdant and beckoning. But then it always does look wonderful. I love this place. It never seems to change. (*Pause.*) I remember when it was just a great muddy plain with not a single plant on the horizon. I thought you were mad.

Reb Yes.

Nick It doesn't last long, does it?

Reb No.

Nick Well. That's it. I guess.

Silence.

Shall we go to bed?

He offers her his hand.

Reb picks up the African carving, goes over to her kitchen bin, lifts the lid, and drops the carving in.

Reb I need to sort out my mind. It's a bit awful isn't it to dream your son did that to you.

She gets the bowl of cornflakes and drops that in the bin. Then the cornflakes, sugar, milk, all the cutlery she can find.

He reminded me so much of you. I wondered if maybe he'd somehow gone crawling under the bed. You know. When he was a little boy. A joke that went horribly wrong.

The bin can't take all the things she's putting into it. But she goes on cramming them in all the same.

I think it was good for him. In a funny sort of way. I think it's given him more confidence. Be good, wouldn't it? (*Pause.*) But what has he done to me? You know what I mean?

Reb locks the French doors.

Nick Lucas! Edwin!

Reb Ah, Lucas. Edwin. You're still expecting them.

Nick unlocks the French doors.

Anything else to go out?

Reb goes to the shelf of pots, takes them all down, looks at them and throws them into the bin. She keeps only one, the one with the gob in it. She rinses it and dries it.

Reb I can never go to bed again.